MOVE MORE STRESS LESS

**Ultimate Guide On How To Release
Stress Through Holistic African Dance.**

Grace Ekall

ABOUT THE AUTHOR

Grace Ekall Grace is originally from Cameroon in central Africa where she founded her dance company and pioneered the Afro-contemporary dance style in Douala, travelled to perform in several countries in Africa; toured in all 10 provinces of Cameroon and 12 cities in France, before arriving in the UK invited by the Arts Council of England to bring her contribution to the dance scene in 2000, visited while being artist in residence in Normandie France. Grace has also taught dance in over 100 schools and colleges in and around Bristol, then her life changed forever. She is a two times breast cancer survivor who climbed Mount Kilimanjaro to raise funds for a local cancer charity in 2010 and pioneered dance for breast cancer patients at Frenchay hospital in 2008 which was championed by ITV News and the BBC. Grace is the creator of a homemade healthy hot sauce range 'Makossa' and founder of Habits That Heal Studio. She uses specific nourishment and holistic African dance as a commodity to improve mental and physical wellbeing. By writing books, - she's now making it possible for more women—regardless of their geographical location—to find the confidence to take control of their health, heal from within, and reach their full potential using - as she puts it, resources they already have.

As seen on Huffpost, Bristol Magazine, Bristol24/7, BBC, Made In Bristol TV, ITV, The Post, BCFM and UJUMA radio.

Table Of Content

My Story

I visited England in 2000 and then moved here in 2001. Being a single mum in a foreign land was very stressful, especially because the black community was significantly different in many ways. People didn't understand me, and I couldn't relate to the deep and complex narrative that surrounded me at the time. I was often told, "You don't get it!" and I guess they were right. Additionally, I initially struggled to express myself properly in English, making it difficult to have meaningful conversations about events in our respective lives. My mum and I used to have long phone conversations about this, but in 2003, I was heartbroken when I lost my mother to a short illness. Then, my sister, only 20 years old, passed away, followed by the passing of my dad. I lost these three close members of my family within 11 months. In 2005, I received devastating news that I have breast cancer, which left me feeling lost, alone at times, and helpless often, back then. However, I realised that I needed to radically change my thoughts when I discovered that I was constantly trapped in a victim mindset. The events in my life were not mere figments of my imagination; they were my reality, and I had valid reasons to feel the way I did. However, my feelings had evolved into a chronic cycle of self-pity. I was living as if cancer was a death sentence and as if I had died along with my family members years ago. Perhaps it was my way of expressing my love for them, but while they rested in peace, I found myself restless and immersed in daily negative torment. Then, one day, I made a decision. Since I am still here and I have a daughter who needs her mother, I might as well strive to live my best life. I can honestly say that, second only to relying on my creator, dance has been my saving grace for both my mental and physical health.

How? That's what I'd like to share with you. I looked at my life and asked myself, "Am I possibly doing things that are making my situation worse? Could I do anything at all that will support my body's natural healing abilities?" The answer to both questions was a resounding YES. I was unknowingly putting my mind and body in danger, and yes, I did have existing resources that could help me make positive changes and improve my health, and I believe you can do the same. Many of you may not know this, but I was born with a severe breathlessness. As a young girl, washing my hair was a stressful task for my mother and me. I would struggle to breathe with my head bent forward towards my feet. Back then, there was no alternative method for washing hair if you were older than a toddler. Breathlessness wasn't recognised as a condition that required treatment. I was simply seen as an "inquisitive child" or even a drama queen. When I was ten years old, I spent a month in the hospital after undergoing a surgical procedure to remove my appendix. The recovery process seemed endless, and one day my mother decided to take me for some fresh air. We walked to the seaside, and with a dramatic tone, she listed the resources available to me and showed me how I could help myself. Despite my bandages needing to stay dry, she suggested I get in the water and do some deep breathing while imagining that the pain in my womb was gone. It was a huge challenge for me that day, but eventually, I found a rhythm in my breathing that made things easier and brought a smile to my face. From that point on, this became my 'thing'... I learned a valuable lesson at a young age: no matter how difficult a situation may seem, there is always some form of power within us to improve it or even change it entirely. Fast forward twenty years or so, with breast cancer diagnosis, I realised that again, I'd already had resources at my disposal that could help change things around for me, so I used those resources and I believe they can help you too. Never allow yourself to become a victim, and Never Give UP!

Instead, take back control of your thoughts and emotions, stay close to nature in every way possible, if you really want to make little changes in your health and life. There are so many things in life that are out of our control, but we have absolute control over two things - our brain, and your breath, meaning that we can alter how they perform. Two amazing high impact pre-installed systems by the greatest engineer of them all. We take our ability to breathe for granted, and we take our amazing brain for granted, because they work like well-oiled machines. The reality is that for these two engines to be highly efficient, so that we can have mental clarity and physical strength - a third component is essential... and that is, movement.

So taking control of your well being means committing to a daily mind and body wellness routine that fits effortlessly into your life, does not create more stress and gets you excited. Stress and negative thoughts can have a debilitating effect on our physical and mental health. Many people struggle with finding effective ways to manage these issues. However, holistic African dance has been found to be a powerful tool for healing and improving well-being. In this book, we will explore the science behind stress and negative thoughts, the benefits of holistic African dance, the whole approach method and how to incorporate it into your life for optimal health. Through holistic African dance, I did find a way out for my mind, body and soul. Today I'm stronger, healthier, leaner and happier. My experience inspired me to share the healing powers of holistic African dance with others. Throughout it all, that lesson again, I have learned that even during the darkest of times, there is always hope and a way to heal. So why choose holistic African dance? Well, holistic health is a practice that takes into account the entire person - their body, mind, and spirit - when striving for optimal health and wellness.

It highlights the significance of maintaining balance in all aspects of one's life, including food, exercise, stress management, and mental health. Holistic health practitioners employ various methods, such as acupuncture, massage, meditation, and herbal remedies, to assist their patients in achieving overall well-being. In my practice, I utilise holistic African dance as the core foundation. By adopting a comprehensive approach to health, individuals can work towards attaining a greater sense of equilibrium, harmony, and vitality in their

Lives.

Image - Google.

Chapter 1

Understanding Stress, Negative Thoughts and the Power of Movement

•What is stress and how does it affect the body?

S tress is a natural response to a perceived threat, challenge, or pressure. It is your body's way of preparing for a fight or flight response, which can be helpful in certain situations.

However, prolonged or chronic stress can have negative effects on your body. When the body perceives stress, it releases hormones such as cortisol and adrenaline. These hormones increase heart rate, blood pressure, respiration frequencies, and redirect the blood flow to muscles and away from the digestive as well as the immune systems. Meaning that it puts the body out of balance of its natural functions. Moving regularly, especially in a particular way that cares for the body, can restore your body's balance in less time than you thought possible. Always keep in mind that chronic stress can lead to anxiety, depression, and sleep disturbances. It can also affect your immune system, making you more susceptible to infections and diseases so these are serious stuff to keep an eye on.

Did you know that stress could also lead to physical symptoms such as headaches, muscle tension on your leg at night, and gastrointestinal problems? Chronic stress has been linked to a variety of health problems, including heart disease, obesity, diabetes and cancer. I found that one way to break the cycle of constant stress is through auto-suggestion, breath work, meditative dance, mindfulness and meditation as well as certain foods. These practices can help regulate your cortisol levels and improve brain function, which help decrease stress and enhance overall sense of wellbeing.

Studies have shown that negative thoughts and negative emotions can alter brain chemistry, resulting in a cycle of negativity and chronic stress. To address this, it is essential to practice various stress management strategies. One such approach is participating in holistic African dance, although other physical activities and therapies can also be effective in reducing negative thoughts and promoting well-being. I often emphasise the connection between movement and mental health, mental clarity, mindset, and emotions because it is a complex yet interconnected relationship.

Our mindset, which refers to how we perceive ourselves and the world, significantly influences our emotions. These emotions, in turn, impact our posture, how we stand, impacts our movement, speech, and overall mental clarity. For instance, a negative mindset can give rise to negative emotions like anxiety or depression, leading to physical tension, poor posture, shallow breathing, and a lack of mental focus. Conversely, a positive mindset can foster positive emotions, relaxed posture, fluid movement, a clear focused mind and a healthier mindset. So in my opinion, although this is not always easy, trust me I'll know, if you commit to fighting negative thoughts with a splash of love towards yourself and others, yes, even that name that just came to your mind, using auto-suggestion, and movement you can make the process of combating negative thoughts easier for yourself.

Self-portrait

I say learn to dance your emotions and move your body as much as you can with intentional happy thoughts. This is important because our brain needs oxygen, fuel and activation...so whatever your state of mind is, that is what you're feeding your brain with.

•Causes of stress and negative thoughts compound

Stress can be caused by a variety of factors including work-related issues, financial worries, relationship problems, including family members, friends, a spouse and health concerns. When stress is ignored, and left unchecked, it can lead to negative thoughts that can escalate and make the situation worse.

Work-related stress can include job insecurity, long hours, a heavy workload and unkind bosses. When work becomes overwhelming, it can lead to feelings of anxiety and frustration. This can also lead to negative thoughts, such as feeling like you are not good enough or that you are failing at your job. Those are not good feelings. A place of work that cares for its employees should have a team building strategy in place as well as wellness policies and stress management activities incorporated into tasks at least once a month. Financial worries can also cause stress. When there is not enough money to pay bills or cover expenses, it can lead to feelings of anxiety and panic. This can cause negative thoughts, such as feeling like you will never get ahead or that you are a failure especially when promises don't come to fruition. Relationship problems can also be a source of stress. When there is conflict or tension in a relationship, it can lead to feelings of anxiety and depression. This can cause negative thoughts, such as feeling like you are unworthy of love or that you are alone in the world. Health concerns can also cause stress. When there is an illness or injury, it can lead to feelings of anxiety and fear. This can cause negative thoughts, such as feeling like you are never going to get better or that you are a burden on others. We could also be stressing about children or grandchildren. Therefore, it seems like everybody needs an effective way to deal with unavoidable stress.

Because as mentioned before when stress is left unchecked, it can make the situation worse and become a self-fulfilling prophecy, causing you to feel even more stressed out and anxious. You then live in this vicious cycle that is difficult to break. Breaking the cycle will require you to identify the cause of your stress and take steps to address it. However, when your stressor is someone or something you love, it can seem like an impossible task to let go of the person or thing. This can be really challenging because the situation is now holding you, your brain, your emotions and your creativity captive without you realising it. The trick is to number one, try not to predict your future.

Because you simply do not know what tomorrow will bring. When you say 'I can't leave, or I can't let go…because…" all you're doing is making assumptions about tomorrow based on yesterday's troubles that are in your subconscious mind; the reality is that you have no clue. Nobody really does. So the smart thing to do is to say 'I can and I will!' and focus on what you can do. Listen to your gut and do what is best for your mental and physical health and you will never go wrong… Number two; quit feeling fearful of what people will think, honestly, people are busy thinking about themselves so they really are not focused on you. Are you disappointed? Also, let go of resentment even if you feel that you have reasons to do so. Resentment is chronic stress on acid. Resentment is a silent killer - choose to walk away instead and heal your soul. Here's another silent killer, guilt. You feel guilty because you might have, should have, could have, may have…all of the above are powerful negative emotions - they are not worthy at all and ridiculously worthless as well. If you cannot fix it, let it be, let it go. Because all these emotions do not serve you or people around you in any way or form. It's basically a bad thing that keeps on giving… And number three, have non-negotiable morning, midday and night daily wellness rituals that keeps your brain cells and body cells on top form. These wellness stations, as I call them, in the morning, midday, and night involve specific movement set for each section of the day, (because you've bought this book, you'll get the video tutorials of these) specific feeding principles and rituals. As you can see, a diet will not cut it, not sustainably. In short, a structured healthy lifestyle is the answer.

•Negative thoughts & the power of movement

Negative thoughts can be a powerful force in our lives unfortunately, and they can impact our overall wellbeing and mental health. These thoughts can be self-critical, self-doubting, and can even escalate into feelings of anxiety and depression. The good news is that one way to combat these negative thoughts is through the power of movement. Whether it is going for a run, taking a dance, Pilates, or yoga class, or even just going for a walk, physical activity has been shown to have a positive impact on our mental health.

Physical activity can also help distract our minds from negative thoughts, allowing us to focus on the present moment and the physical sensations of movement. By incorporating movement into our daily routine, we can develop a sense of accomplishment and empowerment. Setting small goals for physical activity and achieving them can provide a sense of pride and confidence, which can help counteract negative self-talk and self-doubt.

It's important to note that while movement can be beneficial for mental health, it is not a cure-all for mental health issues. Seeking professional support is always recommended. However, incorporating physical activity into our daily routine can be a powerful tool for managing negative thoughts and improving overall mental health.

So, the next time you're feeling overwhelmed by negative thoughts, try taking a walk or doing a few stretches – you might be surprised by the negative impact it can have. Such as contributing to poor mental health, engaging in negative self-talk, feelings of low self-esteem and self-worth. It can also impact your sleep patterns. When we are stressed out or anxious, it can be challenging to fall asleep or stay asleep. Lack of sleep can further exacerbate mental health issues, leading to again, a vicious cycle of poor mental health and poor sleep. Let's revisit the good news... That is, there are steps that we can all take to manage stress and negative thoughts and improve our mental health. You know what I'm going to say... Move! Move! Move! Engaging in regular physical activities, and seeking support from friends, family, or a mental health professional can all be helpful.

•How can you gain the confidence to take back control of negative thoughts and your stress levels?

To gain confidence in taking back the control of negative thoughts and your stress levels, you have access to several strategies that you could implement. These strategies include reframing negative thoughts. Emile Coue, a French psychologist in the 18s introduced a psychotherapy method called autosuggestions that was mocked at the time, but is now used by renowned wellness experts around the world and known as 'affirmation'. He helped his patients going through cancer to use this autosuggestion: "Every day and in every way I'm getting better and better"! Although there are still a lot of debates among health professionals regarding the efficacy of this method still, this can be an effective way to gain the confidence to take back control of negative thoughts. Give yourself permission to believe that things are getting better. You could also try mindfulness, which is the practice of being present and aware of our thoughts, feelings, and surroundings without judgement. By practicing these two techniques, you can become more aware of your negative thoughts patterns and stressors, and learn to observe and acknowledge them without becoming overwhelmed or reactive but active in easing them out of your head. Let me show you how I do this. First thighs first, take a quiz and figure out whether you're a low, moderate or high perceived stress levels individual. Then use 'voice dialogue' in combination with autosuggestion and movement as your go-to stress management. So, if you scored 0 - 13, you have low stress levels. Listen to one of my self-management stress tools, audio no3 - It goes like this:

"Congratulations to me! I have low stress levels, who am I? I'm 'selves' also known as the ego, irrational; and, I am 'self' known as the person within that is whole, and authentic. As 'selves', I judge 'self' all the time, even though 'self', the person within, is always, right, rational, whole. Congratulations to me, I have low stress levels, I'm in 'control', I'm a positive person, I am 'love!' I am 'happiness itself'!

I'm breathing in through my nose, and out through my mouth. I speak to myself and say: Hey! Being worried all the time and going through negative thoughts do not serve me in any way. However, the person within, the authentic and loving 'self,' embraces bad times, sadness, and even tears, because that's life, C'est la vie! I won't beat myself up over feeling hurt, sad, emotional, or worried because, c'est la vie! Instead, I choose to dance these emotions. I express my emotions through a touch, a tap, or a move. Now, let me share a few things that my loved ones do that get on my nerves. I give myself permission to say it aloud! Number one is... Number two is... And number three is... Now, here's what I'd prefer to see happening: number one... number two... and number three... (Silence!) I'm taking a deep breath in through my nose and out through my mouth. I'm committed to maintaining this ritual and relaxing my muscles. I breathe in, and I breathe out, deeply and slowly.

If you scored between 14 and 26, you have moderate stress levels. Allow me to share one of my self-management stress tools, audio number two. It goes like this:

"Congratulations to me for having moderate stress levels. Who am I? I'm 'selves,' also known as the ego, irrational; and I am 'self,' known as the person within, who is whole and authentic. As 'selves,' I judge 'self' all the time, even though... 'self', the person within, is always right, rational, and whole.

Congratulations to me I have moderate stress levels. I am chilled, calm and collected! I'm adaptable; I give back what I gain from people. I care! I don't care!! Do I care??? Maybe I do, maybe I don't. Okay, I'm breathing in through my nose and out through my mouth. I speak to myself and say: Hey! Proud of you! I'm balanced, although super stressed out at times, often having no will to act or react to what's going on around me. I know it might drive you crazy, so I'm now willing to communicate and express my feelings, because this is life. C'est la vie! I'm no longer going to be emotionless, and I'll express myself because, c'est la vie! So, what I'm going to do, I'll dance my emotions. I dance my emotions, with a touch, a tap or move. Here is one annoying thing that I almost always ignore: .... and here is one annoying thing that I don't seem to be capable of ignoring or shaking it off ....So I dance, I dance my emotions, for a balanced reaction, and deal with my triggers in motion!!! (Silence) I'm breathing in through my nose, and out through my mouth. I eat well; I slow down and take a break. I'm making time for myself. Thank you".

If you scored 27- 40, you have high perceived stress levels. Listen to one of my self-management stress tools, audio no1 - It goes like this:

"Congratulations to me, for being honest with myself. I have high perceived stress levels. Who am I? I am 'selves' also known as the ego, irrational; and, I am 'self' known as the person within that is whole, and authentic. As 'selves', I judge 'self' all the time for not keeping up with the to-do-list. Even though 'self', the person within, is always right, rational, and whole. Congratulations to me for acknowledging my high stress levels. I'm restless, I'm judged, I'm judging myself, I'm overwhelmed. There's so much going on, I'm worried, if I don't do xyz, it will be a disaster!!! (Silence) 'I'm breathing in through my nose and out through my mouth. What I'm going to do, I'll work in collaboration with 'self' the person within, and I'm patient with me, I care about what my body is telling me every day. So, I stop, literally stop so I can listen to my body and hear what's actually going on inside, and outwards. Listen to what's actually going on, not perceptions, facts. I stop. I sit down to gain clarity! Because this is life! C'est la vie! To protect my heart from serious health conditions I dance my emotions, I dance my emotions with a touch a tap or a move. I also feel comfortable crying my eyes out - letting go! I'm letting go…Now, I'm setting my intentions for the outcomes that I desire and I'm taking steps to make it happen. I'm ready to compromise or to move on (silence). I'm breathing in through my nose and out through my mouth. I'm making time for my hobbies. I talk things out…I forgive you, I love you. Thank you".

Use the above in conjunction with movement. Movement can support the autosuggestion techniques by helping to reinforce positive thoughts and beliefs through physical actions. For example, incorporating movement such as freedom of motion, deep breathing, stretching, or visualisation exercises can enhance the effectiveness of autosuggestion by reinforcing positive intentions with physical sensations.

Moving your body helps reduce stress and tension, making it easier to focus and concentrate during the autosuggestion process. Engaging in traditional exercise is another effective way to lower stress levels and improve overall mental and physical health. Seeking support from others is also important in regaining confidence and managing negative thoughts and stress. Whether it's talking with a trusted friend, family member, or mental health professional, opening up can provide perspective and alleviate feelings of isolation. Remember that reframing negative thoughts is a powerful technique for gaining control over your mental state. Take slow, deep breaths in through your nose and out through your mouth while practicing this method. By understanding your default response to stress and identifying triggers, you can challenge negative thoughts and replace them with positive and realistic ones. For instance, instead of thinking "I'm not good enough," reframe it as "I am doing all I can, and that is enough." "My health is so bad", reframe that to "My body is doing its very best to heal".

Chapter 2

What Is Holistic African Dance & Its Health Benefits

•First stop: The history and culture of African dance

African dance is a vibrant and diverse art form that has been an integral part of African culture for centuries. The history of African folk dance is deeply rooted in traditional African spirituality and social customs. The origins of African folk dance can be traced back to prehistoric times, when African tribes used dance as a means of communication and worship.

Dance was used to celebrate life events such as births, deaths, weddings, and harvests, as well as to honour the spirits of ancestors and gods, a practice that is still present in folk and traditional dances done in the continent today. As African societies and communities became more complex, dance began to take on a greater social significance. Different regions and tribes developed their own unique styles of dance, each with its own distinct rhythms, movements, and cultural significance.

One of the most well-known forms of African dance is West African dance, which originated in Senegal, Gambia, Guinea, Mali, and the Ivory Coast. West African dance is characterised by its complex rhythms, fast footwork, and energetic movements. Cameroon, located in central Africa, is my native land—a diverse country with over 200 languages and various cultural traditions, including dance. Each ethnic group in Cameroon has its unique dance style, representing its cultural heritage. Some of the popular traditional dances in Cameroon that I enjoyed growing up include Makossa, Bikutsi, Ambassibey, and Assiko.

The Makossa dance is a popular urban dance style that originated from the Douala people. It involves a lot of hip and waist movements. Bikutsi dance, on the other hand, is from the Beti people and features energetic movements of the upper, middle, or lower spine, as well as vibrant percussion beats. The Ambassibey dance, from the Sawa people, includes twill moves, graceful feet and shoulder sequences, and a specific drumming style. The Assiko dance, performed by the Bassa people, showcases incredibly rhythmic hip movements, phrases, and footwork that are unmatched.

Overall, the diverse range of languages, delicious dishes and dances in Cameroon is a testament to the richness of the country's culture and heritage. Many contemporary dance forms, such as jazz, hip-hop, and modern dance, have incorporated elements of African dance into their choreography. Despite its rich history and cultural significance though, African dance has faced significant challenges over the years.

During the colonial era, many African dance traditions were suppressed and even banned by European authorities, who saw them as primitive and uncivilised. Today, however, African dance is experiencing a resurgence in popularity and recognition. African dance troupes are performing around the world, and African dance classes are increasingly common in dance studios and schools. African dance continues to captivate audiences around the world. I would like to give a shout out to the African dance's tutors communities around the world.

•**How African dance in general promotes physical health**

When it comes to African dance, it's fitness at its best. African dance can be a highly energetic cardio and physically demanding art form.

It not only promotes cultural exchange but also has numerous physical benefits. Here are some ways in which African dance can promote physical health. African dance is a high-intensity workout that gets the heart pumping and increases blood flow. It strengthens the heart and can help reduce the risk of heart disease. So great for cardiovascular health. African dance involves a lot of movements that require flexibility, such as leg extensions and sometimes splits. Consistent practice can improve flexibility and reduce the risk of injury. The movements in African dance require the use of various muscle groups at once, including the core, legs, torso, hips and arms. Regular practice can improve muscle tone and increase overall strength. African dance involves complex movements that require coordination between different parts of the body. This can improve overall balance and coordination. African dance is a great way to burn calories and lose weight. The high-intensity movements can help increase metabolic rate and reduce body fat. As well as the fact that dancing is a great way to relieve stress and improve mental health. African dance, in particular, has a rhythmic quality that can be soothing and calming.

African dance requires a lot of energy and stamina, so practicing it regularly can improve endurance and increase the body's ability to perform physical tasks for longer periods. In addition to these physical benefits, African dance not only celebrates the rich cultural heritage of the continent, but also provides an avenue for cultural exchange and appreciation between different communities. It provides a sense of belonging and can therefore be a fun and enjoyable way to stay active and healthy.

The holistic African dance method and our Habits That Heal, theories, principles, rules, and milestones basis are explored throughout this book. And a few infographics are shared as summaries. i.e. - no1

•Holistic African Dance Health Benefits

Holistic African dance is a powerful and expressive art form. Beyond being a form of self-expression, and has many mental health benefits. Firstly, holistic African dance is a great way to reduce stress and anxiety. When you dance, your body releases endorphins, which are natural feel-good chemicals that help to reduce stress and promote relaxation, which you can get from many forms of physical activities.

However, holistic African dance is also about 'connecting to 'self' the person within a core principle in this practice that allows you to dance your emotions, follow your own rhythm, which is a very powerful technique to help calm the mind and reduce feelings of anxiety. Holistic African dance is also a great way to boost self-confidence and self-esteem. Dancing your emotions allows you to be fully present in the moment and express yourself in a way that is unique to you guided by one of the 5 steps and 3 rhythms principles, however, whenever, wherever and no experience needed, no technique required. This can help to build a sense of self-awareness, which can have positive effects on your mental health. Additionally, holistic African dance is also a great way to connect with others and build social connections. Dancing is a communal activity that brings people together, and holistic African dance is no exception.

When you dance with others, you build a sense of camaraderie and connection that can help combat feelings of loneliness and isolation, especially for people living alone. Another amazing mental health benefit of holistic African dance is that it can improve cognitive function. Practicing holistic African dance requires you to memorise emotional waves, choose rhythms, transition to different rhythms, transfer weight, memorise steps, and stay in rhythm. In holistic African dance, freedom of movement does not mean dancing aimlessly; you learn to coordinate your movements with your thoughts, music, a silence, beat, or tempo...You also choose what to focus on and when to move, following your own rhythm.

Participants are encouraged to set up their intentions using the five basic steps as a guide. This can help improve your memory, focus, and attention span as well, all of which are important for good mental health. I'll say that holistic African dance is a great way to challenge yourself and build resilience. Dancing your emotions is about mental focus, which can be difficult to maintain over long periods of time. By pushing yourself to overcome these challenges, you can build resilience and develop a strong sense of self-discipline that can help you overcome other challenges in your life. Holistic African dance has many mental health benefits that make it a great activity for people of all ages and backgrounds. Whether you are looking to reduce stress, build self-confidence, connect with others, improve cognitive function, or build resilience, holistic African dance can be a powerful tool for improving your mental health and well-being.

•The Difference between Moving And Exercising

Movement involves being in motion and active throughout the day, such as, taking the stairs instead of the lift, walking to work instead of driving, or doing household chores with the intention of getting the most out of them. Doing a little dance now and then throughout the day. Exercising, on the other hand, involves setting aside dedicated time for physical activity, such as going for a run, lifting weights, or attending a fitness class. While both are beneficial for overall health, exercising 3 times a week for example allows for a more structured and intense workout, while moving regularly helps to maintain an active lifestyle throughout the day. Because holistic African dance is inspired by ancient wisdom, animals, plants, and natural phenomena, such as rain, wind, and thunder. These expressions reflect the belief that everything in the world is interconnected and that humans are an integral part of the natural order, which can help you put things into perspective and you can never run out of inspiration. Exercising is not for everybody, moving is for everybody. Moving every day is incorporating physical activity into our daily routines.

While exercise is also important for overall health, moving every day is smart because it will help you avoid being sedentary, which can have negative health consequences if you sit all the time and do not have enough physical activity in your life. Additionally, incorporating movement into our daily routines can make it easier to maintain healthy habits long-term. Just remember that this is not always easy. Be kind to yourself and enjoy your process of improvement or change.

i.e. - no2

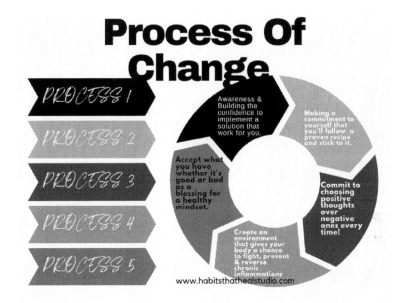

Process Of Change

PROCESS 1

PROCESS 2

PROCESS 3

PROCESS 4

PROCESS 5

Awareness & Building the confidence to implement a solution that work for you.

Making a commitment to yourself that you'll follow a proven recipe and stick to it.

Accept what you have whether it's good or bad as a blessing for a healthy mindset.

Commit to choosing positive thoughts over negative ones every time!

Create an environment that gives your body a chance to fight, prevent & reverse chronic inflammations

www.habitsthathealstudio.com

Incorporating Holistic African Dance Into Your Life

•Finding a dance community

Incorporating therapeutic dance forms into your life can be a transformative and enriching experience. These types of dance styles are not just a physical exercise, but holistic practice that connects the mind, body, and spirit. Here are some tips on how to get started and find a dance community. If you're passionate about dance as a healing tool, Start by researching local studios and classes that offer therapeutic dance classes. Look for reviews and recommendations from others who have taken these classes. Many studios offer trial sessions or introductory packages, so take advantage of those opportunities to see if the dance style and community is a good fit for you. In addition to regular classes, many studios and dance organisations offer workshops and events that focus on specific aspects of therapeutic dance or bring in guest teachers.

Attending these events can be a great way to deepen your understanding of the dance style and connect with other dancers in that community. Social media can be a great way to connect with other people who dance for a purpose in your area. Look for Facebook groups or Instagram accounts dedicated to Dance therapy, or dance psychotherapy and reach out to other dancers to ask for recommendations or to see if they want to attend a class or event with you. When it comes to holistic African dance, it is not just about the physical movement, it's also more about the feelings, the emotions and 'self' the person within. It's about being aware of the process of change. Understanding that it takes time. Learning to show up for your brain and body, so if you can make a commitment to yourself to attend these classes regularly, and consider practicing what you learn at home or attending workshops or retreats to deepen your understanding of those healing dance styles. Incorporating holistic African dance into your life can be a rewarding and a transformative experience that helps you understand and love your body more. That's something many don't do. Promoting self-love is absolutely essential in holistic African dance so you can gain the confidence to take back control of your health so you can give your best to your loved ones. This means treating yourself with kindness and compassion, and recognising that you are worthy of love and care. This can also be done through self-care practices such as reading Holy Scriptures, taking a relaxing bath, breathing consciously, practicing gratitude, or setting boundaries with others. So, gaining the confidence to take control of your health is foremost about taking full responsibility for your health and wellbeing, or a lack thereof! It requires a combination of positive thinking, conscious movement, and managing worries and overwhelm, and running a self-love campaign, daily. By incorporating these practices into your daily routine, you can begin to believe in your ability to make positive changes and improve your overall health and well-being. Now!

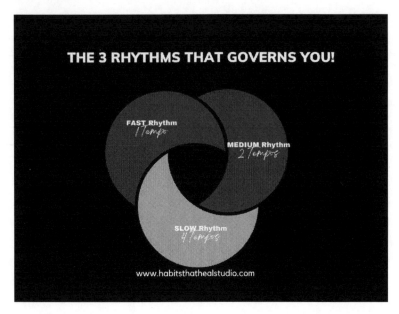

Rhythm of exhaustion - **SLOW "Tempo".** Rhythm of 'loveness' time spent with loved ones - **MEDIUM "Tempo"**& Rhythm of speed & chaos - **FAST "Tempo".** Learn to dance your emotions, using these "tempos" in conjunction with specific conscious breathing. You can choose a rhythm or tempo depending on how you feel at that moment.

Chapter 3

LET'S DANCE! -**The Diaphragmatic Breathing Technique Dance ~**

By incorporating diaphragmatic breathing techniques into our holistic African dance practice, we can deepen our connection to ourselves and the world around us. Here are three holistic African dance combos that work well with diaphragmatic breathing, which is a deep breathing exercise that fully engages the diaphragm. Our lungs expand and contract with the help of the diaphragm, a large muscle that sits below the lungs. The majority of people are shallow breathers, inhaling through their mouth, and unconsciously holding their breath which compromise the natural breathing patterns.

Causes of this shift could be triggered by several sources of anxiety such as reacting to pollution, temperature, or a forceful concentration on a task that is challenging and of course health conditions. When this happens, we need to relearn how to breathe properly. If we're aiming to achieve diaphragmatic breathing also known as belly breathing, the ideal position for this will be the deep squats, I mean all the way down - This exercise is so great and strengthens lower back, glutes, quads, hamstrings, as well as helping with stability and balance. According to research, 80% of the population have breathing dysfunction. And because the poor breathing has been developed throughout the years, it becomes a bad habit that is challenging to change. I have been using Cameroonian traditional dances paired with specific breathing techniques to make breathing properly fun and healing.

The Assiko Dance ~

The Assiko is a popular dance from Cameroon that is characterised by its energetic and lively movements. Great for diaphragmatic breathing. To perform the Assiko, start by standing with your feet shoulder-width apart, (or feet together if more comfortable) and your arms at your sides. Begin by taking a deep breath and exhaling slowly, focusing on filling your lungs with air and then releasing it slowly as you go into deep squats all the way down. Keep your feet flat if you're a beginner, and as you progress go on the ball of your feet. As you inhale again, lift your arm above your head and begin to sway your hips from side to side. As you exhale, lower your arm and bring your feet together. Beginners, roll up the spine to be in a standing position. Advance, from being on the ball of your feet start rising up slowly coming to the standing position, moving still, soft on your knees. Continue to repeat this movement, focusing on your breath and the rhythm of the music and switching arms.

The Ambassibey Dance ~

The Ambassibey is a traditional dance from Cameroon that is performed to celebrate the harvest season. It is a slow and graceful dance that is ideal for practicing diaphragmatic breathing also. To perform the Ambassibey, start by standing with your feet hip-width apart and your arms at your sides. Take a deep breath in and exhale slowly, focusing on your breath and the sensation of your body moving right foot heel on the ground, slide foot on the right hand side as you open your arms shoulder length. As you inhale again, lift your right foot off the ground and extend it in front of you, balancing on your left foot. Hold this pose for a few seconds, and then slowly lower your foot back to the ground. Repeat this movement with your left foot, focusing on your breath and the sensation of your body moving.

The Djembe Dance ~

The Djembe is a West African drum that is often used in traditional dance performances throughout the continent including Cameroon. It is a powerful and energetic dance that is perfect for practicing diaphragmatic breathing. To perform the Djembe, start by standing with your feet shoulder-width apart and your arms at your sides. Begin by taking a deep breath and exhaling slowly, focusing on the sensation of your breath moving through your body. As you inhale again, lift your right foot off the ground and stomp it back down, simultaneously raising your right arm above your head and striking a pretend Djembe should be placed in front of you or on your right-hand side. For the polarity technique, use your left arm to assist your right arm by placing the left hand on top of the right one. As you exhale, lower your right arm and bring your foot back to the ground. Repeat this movement with your left foot and right hand supporting each other, while focusing on your breath, the rhythm of the music, your thoughts, or simply silence.

Now, stomp on the balls of your feet and follow the music or move in silence. Cross and uncross your feet in double tempo, (Croiser, changer step), alternating from one foot to the other. Keep both arms in the air, moving each arm in sync with the opposite foot. These dance moves with polarity are beneficial for your brain's memory and can unlock your body's electromagnetic field, opening doors to a range of freedom of movement you may not have realised you possess.

Incorporating diaphragmatic breathing techniques into holistic African dance practice can deepen your connection to yourself and the world around you. By practicing the Ambassibey, Assiko, and Djembe dance steps, you can improve your breathing, increase body awareness, and enjoy the numerous benefits of this powerful dance form....This is the first step of the 5 - a strong and deliberate foot stomp that creates grounding energy.More on this later.

How To Prepare For A Holistic African Dance Session ~

Preparing for a holistic African dance session involves taking care of your feet, body, mind, and soul. Here are some tips to help you get ready for this transformative experience, just like any physical activity, make sure you drink plenty of water before, or rather, sipping some water during, and after the class to stay hydrated. Choose loose, breathable clothing that allows you to move freely. Avoid tight or restrictive clothing that could limit your movement or make you feel self-conscious. Take some time to stretch your muscles, breathe consciously and warm up your body before the class begins.

To prevent injury and improve your flexibility, it's important to prepare both your mind and body. Be open to learning new things and give yourself permission to explore unfamiliar territory. Practice mindfulness and gratitude for being able to attend the class, as this will help you focus and clear your mind. It will also make it easier for you to connect with your own rhythm, the music, and the movements on a deeper level.

Take some time to learn about the background and cultural origins of the dance you will be practicing. This will help you gain a better understanding of the meaning and significance behind the movements. Keep in mind that sometimes there may not be a specific meaning, and that's okay too.

You can interpret it in your own way and make it meaningful to you.

Use this opportunity to connect with others in the class. Holistic African dance is often performed in a group setting, so take advantage of the chance to build community and form connections. Approach the class with a positive attitude and an open mind. Allow yourself to be present in the moment and embrace the experience.

By following these tips, you can prepare yourself for a transformative and empowering holistic African dance session. During the class, we dance barefoot and utilise African dance techniques, including using our heels, the balls of our feet, and the soles. Remember to listen to your body, work with not against your body, it's appropriate to say go with the flow here, and have fun! Be ready to spend at the very least 5 minutes working on the soles of your feet in this practice. For me, feet are the most important body part. Did you know that one quarter of your bones are in your feet? Yep! Your foot and ankle has over 100 muscles, tendons and ligaments, 33 joints and 26 bones.

It's a very complex mechanical structure. Your feet produce up to half a unit of perspiration each day with its 250,000 sweat glands on average. So, keeping your feet locked in your shoes all the time is not good. Central organs such as the stomach, and spinal column as well as the kidney, lungs, liver are on your feet and the toes directly connected with the brain and its organs. Ancient wisdom! Holistic African dance also uses specific hands expressions and fingers pressure points. I became very interested in hands at a very young age prompted by comments my friends and later on adults say about them. That is a story for another time.

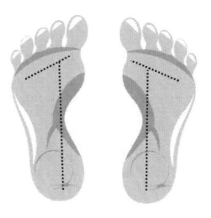

Image - Habits That Heal Studio

Combining dance with other wellness practices

Because holistic African dance is a powerful practice that engages the mind, body, and soul in a dynamic and expressive way, combining it with other wellness practices can enhance its benefits and provide a more comprehensive approach to overall well-being.

One way to combine holistic African dance with other wellness practices is by integrating mindfulness techniques. By incorporating mindfulness into holistic African dance, you can deepen your connection to the movements, rhythm, thoughts, sounds, silence, and music, and enhance your overall sense of awareness. This can also help you focus your thoughts and intentions.

Another way to combine holistic African dance with other wellness practices is through the use of breath work. Breathing exercises can help regulate your nervous system, reduce stress and anxiety, and increase feelings of relaxation and calm. By incorporating breath work into holistic African dance, you can experience tangible improvements in your overall health and sense of well-being.

In addition, holistic African dance can be combined with practices such as yoga, meditation, and tai chi to create a more comprehensive wellness practice. These practices all involve movement, breath work, and mindfulness, and can complement holistic African dance in a special powerful way.

Holistic African dance can also be combined with healing practices such as massage, acupuncture. Holistic African dance can also be combined with nutritional practices. Specific nourishment foods combined with holistic African dance can support your body's natural healing processes and enhance your overall sense of well-being. You can also use holistic African dance as a form of gentle exercise to support physical health and well-being.

Chapter 4

Success Stories

•Personal stories of people who have used holistic African dance to heal from stress and negative thoughts

L et me tell you about three women who found themselves struggling with stress and negative thoughts. They each discovered the healing power of holistic African dance and began to attend classes regularly.

As they danced to the rhythm of their heart and sometimes drums, they felt a sense of release and freedom even though these sessions were all done online. Not in person. With each step, they shed their worries and fears, and embraced the present moment. Over time, they became more grounded, centred, and confident. They felt a deep connection to themselves, each other, and the world around them. And so, they continued to dance, grateful for the healing and transformation it brought to their lives. They are still joining my private sessions today. Marie discovered the healing power of holistic African dance through her own personal experiences. After struggling with depression and anxiety, she got in touch and really turned into holistic African dance as a way to connect with her body and release negative emotions. Through this practice, she discovered a newfound sense of empowerment and healing. She now shares her knowledge and passion for holistic African dance with others, helping them unlock the transformative power of this ancient practice. Women face various struggles in life that often go unaddressed, leading them to seek out holistic African dance as a means of healing and self-expression. Some common challenges include societal pressure to conform to unrealistic beauty standards, health issues considered taboo, poor posture, and systemic inequality. Holistic African dance offers a safe and supportive space for women to connect with their bodies, release emotional trauma, and embrace their authentic selves. Additionally, it fosters community building through movement and rhythm.

Throughout the five years of establishing this practice, holistic African dance has proven to be a powerful tool for women in coping with stress and negative thoughts. The rhythmic movement and music can also induce a meditative effect, calming the mind and reducing anxiety. Men can give it a go as well.

•Testimonials from African dance instructors and therapists

Here are a couple of testimonials from holistic African dance instructors and therapists:

•   "As a holistic practice instructor, and a student of Grace, I have seen firsthand the transformative power of holistic African dance practice. It allows individuals to connect with their body, mind, and spirit in a way that is truly unique. Through movement, we are able to release stress, express ourselves, and tap into our inner power. I am honoured to share this practice with my students now, and witness their growth and transformation." Miranda. W

•   "As a therapist who incorporates holistic African dance into my practice, I have found that it can be an incredibly effective way to address both physical and emotional issues. Grace's 5 steps and 3 rhythms of holistic African dance have a way of unlocking emotions and releasing the tension in the body. It can be a powerful tool for healing and growth." Rebecca .S

Chapter 5

How to Manage Stress

To be successful in managing stress, a combination of factors is required. These include getting enough rest, taking care of your body, practicing conscious breathing, stretching, engaging in regular movement, and consuming immune-supporting foods. So, how can you handle a stressful situation in a way that prevents it from worsening? Well, breathe! Whatever is currently challenging your emotions cannot physically break you.

Emotionally, yes! Physically, no. However, since it can affect your breathing pattern, it's important to take this seriously and find a way to manage the stress first. As long as you are still standing, and if you genuinely want things to improve, they can. It's easier said than done, I know! Naturally, you want to see things improve, but it's hard... yes, it is! But remember, my dear, you are capable of overcoming difficult challenges. I'm confident that you've tackled some tough situations in the past, so you can certainly handle this one also. Here are a few more tips to manage stress, first things first, be aware that drugs, alcohol, cigarettes and other substances can be stress triggers, and breathing pattern 'compromisers'... so, try harder to quit.

The good news is that having a ritual, movement routine can reduce the risk of chronic stress and improve your breathing pattern. I'll know! I've spoken about this so many times. As a child, and young adult I struggled with shortness of breath. For a very long time I forgot I ever had that problem until going through trementous treatment, I started struggling with my breath again and even though I've managed to regulate a healthy breathing pattern for myself, whenever I begin to feel stressed out, I notice changes in the way I breathe. Holistic African dance forces me to breathe properly so that's my go to solution.

Photo - Berny Beroh

Now about the stressors, learn to say 'no!', don't ever say 'yes' to anything without thinking about it first. We often say 'yes' first, then, realise we can't really do whatever we promised we'll do...or do it begrudgingly because we made a promise. I challenge you to unapologetically practice self-health throughout the day. Say 'no' to at least one thing a day. It could be someone demanding something of you or you leaping without thinking into a situation that doesn't necessarily need you. And next thing you know you're dealing with an overload of things to do. I suggest a '4 stops' throughout the day to people who work with me, these 'stops' are 'conscious movement time', and time to take multiple breaths, think and set your intentions for the next part of your day. Auto-suggest good energy, vibrations, and be more sociable. Soooo healing! In addition, I'm thinking, most of all, when you make that stop, acknowledge your emotions, shift your thoughts, change your breath, forgive yourself and forgive others.

It's time to dance! Okay, try dancing these simple African dance steps - effortless African dance... :))-simple routine to learn - Try to remember it and show us how you do it with or without music. It was live with DJembe drums recorded on the phone from far away, so the sound is not great.https://youtu.be/m5ZtZs1SujQ Your tasks is to locate the 'drum's calls' for you to change the move, try to apply yourself to the 'hesitation steps', the polarity phrase, the hips work, abs work & side steps combo, then a complex sequence of legs & arms. Brainwork, weight transfer & bold arm movements, twill, and whole-body motion & last but not least, stopping at the same time as the Proofread and edited version: drums! Amusez-Vous Bien! If you have any questions, don't hesitate to ask. Now let's talk about dance as a whole, and its various aspects.

First, let's define 'dance leaders.' Note that we are not referring to 'dance leads,' but leaders in different roles. I categorise them as 'dance leaders as callers,' 'dance leaders as facilitators,' and 'dance leaders as choreographers.'

'Callers' are leaders of traditional dances. They provide instructions to the participants on how to perform specific dance combinations. These instructions have been passed down for generations, sometimes for hundreds of years. In the culture of the Sawa people in Cameroon, the dance leader caller gives instructions while the participants are already in motion. The dancers then adjust the rhythm, direction, or pace based on these instructions. In other cultures, the caller provides instructions before each dance section is performed. It's important to note that callers are not choreographers. They do not create new moves or sequences.

Choreographers, on the other hand, are dance leaders who create movement, routines, formations, sequences, visual stories, scenes, and even choose or create the music for the piece. As a former choreographer myself, I have created over 80 dance pieces. Choreographies throughout my career for my Dance Company, musicians back home, and theatre companies in Cameroon and

France. A choreographer becomes a 'caller' of their choreography as soon as the dance steps are learned by the students, participants, or dance crew to guide them to the right changes, formations and techniques. They do so before the dance sequence, during and after. Although a choreographer can also be a facilitator, I use the term here in a specific context.

A dance-leader facilitator for me, is in the context of therapeutic dance. They are neither choreographers nor 'callers', rather, they are qualified 'emotional space holders'

They create a safe environment where participants can freely express themselves through movement. However, this practice can be very dangerous if the dance facilitator leader is not qualified to lead these sessions. To be a dance therapist, one needs at least a degree in the subject. So, being a dance teacher does not automatically make your dance sessions holistic, therapeutic, or psychotherapeutic. Nonetheless, it's never too late to obtain the necessary qualifications. It's important to note that a dance therapist is not the same as a dance psychotherapist. To become a dance psychotherapist, a higher education at the master's level is required. While dance as a whole can stimulate the four main happiness emotions

(Serotonin, Dopamine, Endorphins, and Oxytocin) and improve mood, holistic and therapeutic dance practices delve much deeper. Therefore, it is crucial to have a solid understanding of what you're doing. You cannot simply wing it. Apologies for any disappointment!

Now let us discuss holistic African dance. As mentioned earlier, this healing dance form was created after a breast cancer diagnosis. I was in so much pain that I couldn't go to the gym or dance as I used to. Consequently, I developed a self-soothing dance that is not considered dance psychotherapy and does not require the assistance of a dance therapist. I like to think of holistic African dance as a as a mental and physical self-care dance, a dance that guides you into breathing consciously and empowers you to be the most qualified health expert out there, when it comes to your own health. In holistic African dance sessions, short and bespoke choreographies can be created by all participants only if the session influenced by their involvement, leads to that. It's entirely up to the students, participant or client. This methodology is based on 5 simple steps and 3 rhythms that are relatable and fun. I've received 23 questions at the moment I'm writing this book and I'll answer the top 3 here now.

What is holistic African dance?

Holistic African dance is a type of dance that emphasises the connection between the mind, body, and soul as well as practising 5 specific breathing techniques. It is rooted in African dance techniques and incorporates movements that reflect the natural environment, animals, and daily life as well as specific breath work, and has its own principles, rules and philosophy. The dance can be done in silence, use healing music or be accompanied by live drumming and aim to empower individuals to gain back control of their wellbeing.

How can holistic African dance help with my stress levels?

Holistic African dance can help reduce stress levels by providing tools that help you leverage autosuggestion techniques, breathing techniques and energetic outlet for mental and physical well-being, allowing for an escape from daily stressors, and promoting mindfulness and relaxation through the use of rhythmic movements led by you or using calming music. Additionally, the social aspect of dancing with others can also provide a sense of community and support.

Is holistic African dance a performing dance style?

No, holistic African dance is not a performing dance style, it incorporates emotions, breath work, various aspects of African culture, including music, storytelling, and auto-suggestion to empower 'self' the person within. The practice emphasises the connection between the mind, body, and soul, so it is all about the individuals. Having said that, it can be used as or in a performing dance number if a choreographer so chooses.

Here is the first dance step and principles of this innovative dance practice to up-lift your general well-being & work towards improving your mood and health on the GO! Arms toward the ceiling start stomping one foot at a time in the 'hesitation' step and slide it back, retrieving your foot as if you changed your mind about stepping forward...accompanied by both arms...alternate feet, then do the 'croiser/changer' steps mentioned previously. Don't forget to breathe from your belly.

I run Holistic African Dance, classes, courses & Workshops and the Holistic 5 Steps RETREAT as well as a morning ritual that helps you dance your way to healing. Healing your mind, body and soul with this energising morning ritual that utilises ancient and afro-based healing techniques. If you are looking for a feel-good gentle workout to improve your wellbeing, if you want to express your emotions through dance, Heal your body with movement, holistic African dance is not just a form of escapism, it's the perfect remedy that will set you up for the day, week, and months to come. Maybe you simply love moving your body or it needs a little pick-me-up - this should do the trick. Holistic African dance is a self-care therapeutic way to process our emotions, many of which we might struggle tapping into normally. This powerful form of dance can help to reduce stress levels, alleviate symptoms of anxiety and depression, and boost self-esteem. Our unique combination of positive psychology, auto-suggestion, African dance-based techniques and movement will introduce you to a different kind of dance class that will help you to let go. If you're a holistic practitioner let me know if you'd like to incorporate holistic African dance into your practice, and I'll surely show you how.

Holistic African Dance Courses, What to expect...

You can expect tips to a proper roadmap to wellness, weaved into 3 key parts. We introduce the class with an overview of African dance and its history, as well as an explanation of the holistic principles that underpin the practice. It's all about getting ready before the work begins. And because stress is a considerable factor to our health struggles in general, and it can hinder our health improvement efforts, you'll get tips, and hacks on the quickest way to solve this, gain awareness and see possibilities. We're big on why it helps to be aware that - following a regular morning and night cycle for getting up and going to bed for example can have numerous benefits for both physical and mental health as mentioned earlier. Our bodies are naturally tuned to this cycle, and maintaining a consistent sleep schedule can improve sleep quality, boost energy levels, and enhance overall well-being, something that many ignore unfortunately. During my immersive workshops and mini-retreats, we speak about how important it is to establish a routine and how this can help improve productivity, focus, and mood throughout the day, therefore reducing stress and anxiety especially when combining movement in our routine. However, exercise can be daunting. There's a growing need for holistic healing tools that are accessible, culturally relevant, authentic to people and effective. We go deep into ancient wisdom secrets behind these principles for early rise, bed time and movement, how this relates to African culture and dance are significant aspects of daily wellness routines that involve continuous movement throughout the day. This exploration of holistic African dance values emphasises their practicality and the potential for leading healthier and more balanced lives. It also underscores the importance of self-commitment and offers strategies to avoid negative emotions such as guilt, shame, and helplessness. Personally, I understand the destructive impact of these emotions, as they nearly ruined my life during a period of anger, confusion, and frustration. Given the risks associated with going to the gym due to the potential development of Lymphedema after my mastectomy, I sought alternative ways to stay active. Dancing became my go-to solution, providing me with constant movement and joy. Soft exercises at home, dancing, laughter, tapping, and trampolining became my favourite activities to maintain an active lifestyle. Also, I view breathing as an art form, and a conscious physical activity. Yes, I know! And there's a right way to breathe when it comes to the Holistic African Dance practice and I will be sharing the 5 conscious breathing techniques that I use. I'll share how each breath works and is used in holistic African dance in connection to the HAD 5 Steps and 3 Rhythms method, created with busy female entrepreneurs and mums in mind and how it can be used on the go! The holistic African dance method is all about mindset, emotions, feelings, movement, clarity and connection. What is in this book is my personal experience of using holistic African dance as a means of healing trauma, it's a powerful testimony to the effectiveness of this practice. We have to acknowledge that many people struggle with trauma, anxiety, and other emotional challenges, and holistic African dance can provide a unique perspective on how this practice and ancient wisdom can be used to address these issues in a holistic and empowering way. This leads us to the daily routine done in 5 steps & 3 rhythms. The holistic African dance's morning, midday and night routines.

Morning routines are another thing I feel have become increasingly popular in recent years, with many people incorporating practices such as meditation, exercise, and journaling into their daily rituals. These activities can help set the tone for the day ahead, providing a sense of calm and clarity as we   navigate   our   busy   lives.

Ancient wisdom, such as that found in Ayurvedic practices, African rituals and Chinese medicine, also emphasises the importance of morning routines, with practices that can sometimes step away from the physical and promote things such as tongue scraping and oil pulling believed to promote overall health and wellbeing. As you're well aware, wellbeing is not just about fitness and certainly not about dieting it's mostly about deeper care of yourself! So, the Holistic African Dance whole approach methodology... 5 steps, moves, 5, traditional dances from Cameroun, 5 steps milestones, mindset, movement and munching as well as the 3 rhythms that accompany the above, are principles that I suggest you check out. There are so many ways in which holistic African dance can be used as a healing tool for trauma, stress, and other emotional and physical challenges. The starting point is dancing your emotions. Gaining the confidence to take back control of your health and wellbeing so you can heal the body and soul. Holistic African dance principles are rooted in the belief that the body and soul are interconnected, and that dance can be a powerful tool for healing both. Confidence is a key component of this practice, as it allows participants to fully embody the movement and connect with their inner selves.

By building confidence through dance, individuals can gain a deeper understanding and acceptance of themselves, leading to a greater sense of overall well-being. Let's go through this again, the five literal steps of the holistic African dance method that has 5 core keys that will be introduced to you in a moment.

These dance steps represent both the physical movements and the overarching philosophy of holistic African dance. They serve as the fundamental building blocks of this dance form and are utilised in various ways across different styles and health protocols. The first step, known as 'Croiser/changer & stump', involves a strong and deliberate foot stomp that creates a sense of being grounded. It signifies taking a firm stand and gaining the confidence to take control of something that is important to your well-being, such as your health. The second step is the 'shuffle', a quick and light movement that embodies agility and motion. It represents the act of rebuilding whatever has been undone. The third step is the 'kick', a powerful and dynamic movement that symbolises strength and energy. It's about awakening yourself, motivating yourself to keep moving forward, and reminding yourself to be grateful and appreciative of what you already have instead of dwelling on what you lack. Lastly, the fourth step is the 'twist', which involves a twisting motion of the hips, and moving parts of the body in isolation and is used to express fluidity and grace as well as the flow of your intentions. Finally, the fifth step is the 'jump', which is a high-energy movement that represents joy and celebration and intentionally leaping into the unknown. It's about embracing your body and constantly taking a leap of faith because 'c'est la vie'! That's life! These are combined with arms movement. We dive into these in class and explore how they can work in your healthy lifestyle plans. Now, let's repeat the three rhythms of holistic African dance mentioned in chapter two. The first rhythm is the 'Saw rhythm', rhythm of exhaustion, which is characterised by deep and resonant drumming, instrument or sound. SLOW tempo (also represents the morning after the night before...hangover, tired).

The second rhythm is the 'Leke' rhythm, rhythm of 'loveness' of the time spent with loved ones, which is a medium beat, sometimes fast-paced rhythm that is used in all kinds of joyous occasions and ceremonies. MEDIUM. Finally, the third rhythm is the 'Bant rhythm', rhythm of speed and chaos which is a high-energy rhythm that is often used in hips and chest movement for celebration and social gatherings. FAST (it also represents the fast pace of a busy and chaotic life) these rhythms are part of our everyday lives whether we like it or not.

Habits That Heal Weekend RETREAT: Call To Book.

Methodology, philosophy, principles, dances and techniques

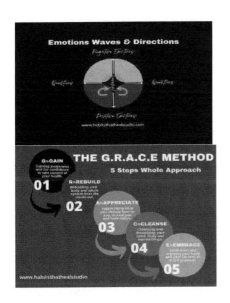

5 Points Bulb Milestone

The 5 Keys mentioned above, the acronym G.R.A.C.E - gain, rebuild, appreciate, cleanse and embrace. These steps are both dance steps and principles of a healthy lifestyle. They are executed in three rhythms and breathe work featured in this book. So the basic implementation of the Slow and medium rhythms is using the diaphragmatic breathing as you're using this pace. Begin by standing with your feet shoulder-width apart and take a deep breath in through your nose, expanding your diaphragm. The dance move for this is the negative and positive emotion waves. Step number one, we will be acknowledging the feet then dropping all the way down to a deep squat. As you exhale through your mouth, begin to move your body in a fluid and rhythmic manner, hands wildly opened as you incorporate either the negative or the positive emotion waves.

Please note that in holistic African dance practices, positive emotions are expressed downward, while negative emotions are expressed upward. Continue to focus on your breath and the movements of your body, allowing yourself to fully immerse in the holistic experience of African dance and diaphragmatic breathing as you transfer your weight from one foot to the other. Now, let's explore autosuggestion and gaining confidence to regain control of our health. It is all about being conscious of the power of your emotions, thoughts, and breathe, as they are interdependent and can change your beliefs. Negative emotions should be directed upward (due to feelings of being lost and confused), while positive emotions should be directed down (because of feeling grounded - legs apart, and knees bent) Hands opened, and reaching out as far as you can go to your left with your left arm and to your right with your right arm are 'QUESTIONS' and scooping air in front of you with both arms is finding ANSWERS and bringing this energy to your chest, belly, neck, arm or face is UTILISING what serves you.

Self-portrait

Practice pursed-lip breathing by following these steps: Inhale deeply through your nose, then exhale slowly through pursed lips, as if you are blowing out through a straw. This technique can help control shortness of breath. To add movement to the exercise, find a comfortable and quiet space where you can sit or stand with a straight back and relaxed shoulders. Begin by taking a deep breath in through your nose, filling your lungs with air.

After that, squeeze your lips together as if you were going to whistle, and exhale slowly through your mouth. Remember to incorporate movement into the exercise every time. Continue to breathe in deeply through your nose and exhale slowly through your pursed lips. As you breathe, you may want to try incorporating some gentle movements or dance of your own, allowing your body to move and flow with your breath. This can help promote relaxation and reduce stress, especially if you include positive autosuggestion to visualise the desired outcomes. It's worth noting that pursed-lip breathing has several health benefits...it can help improve breathing efficiency and reduce shortness of breath. It can also help decrease the work of breathing and promote relaxation. Additionally, it may be beneficial for individuals with chronic obstructive pulmonary disease (COPD) or asthma to help manage symptoms. Step number two, it's about playing with weight transfer and challenging the body more and more. It's all about rebuilding the Body from the inside out, which includes specific nutrients. And step number three, appreciating all the resources that you have already. Hip movement and moving the body in isolation. Try alternate nostril breathing. It is a little bit tricky to move your hips while implementing this breathing technique but if you manage to find a rhythm that suits you it will do wonders to your body. Okay, close one nostril with your finger, inhale through the other nostril, then close that nostril and exhale through the first nostril. Repeat on the other side. The hip roll is towards the side of the nose that is breathing out. This can help balance your energy, calm your mind and help with your cognitive as well as your vibration, and flow. If you are looking for ways to improve energy, vibration, and flow in your life. Engaging in regular holistic African dance, conscious breathing is choosing oxygen over toxins. Conscious movement is a meditative dance. Conscious Digestion is working in collaboration with your bodily natural function in fusion with nature electro & magnetic waves, Energy and vibrations, mindfulness and meditation can be helpful in promoting positive energy and flow.

Additionally, surrounding yourself with positive and supportive people and engaging in activities that bring you joy and fulfilment can also contribute to a more positive and vibrant experience.

Step number four, is to cleanse your body and the previous step is doing that but now is time to add a rigorous stopping of the feet and intricate combination of the torso and feet movement or any part of the upper body and the feet. Your ego will have a few things to say about this, so acknowledge the 'selves', which is your ego, and prepare to cleanse your mind and body. Finally in step number five, embrace your body and enjoy your life and you are going to have plenty of tools here in the habits that heal studio to do just that. Experiment with resistance breathing. Use an actual straw or a breathing device to create resistance while exhaling. This can help strengthen your respiratory muscles. Four, seven, eight breathing technique. Breathe in for 4, hold for 7 and out for 8. There is some evidence to suggest that practicing breath-holding exercises can improve lung function and increase oxygen efficiency in the body. It can also help reduce stress and anxiety by promoting relaxation.

However, breath holding should only be done in a controlled environment.

CONCLUSION

Moving more and stressing less is the aim, as it can significantly impact your overall health and well-being. By including physical activity in your daily routine and learning effective stress management techniques, you can enhance your mood, increase your energy levels, and reduce the risk of chronic diseases. Remember to start with small steps, stay consistent, and celebrate your progress along the way. With dedication and commitment, you can achieve a more balanced life.

This book has explored the numerous benefits of incorporating holistic African dance into your daily routine as a way to move more and stress less. This dance form emphasises the connection between the mind, body, and soul, providing a unique and powerful method to improve your physical health, mental well-being, and overall quality of life. It empowers you to regain control over your own health and wellbeing. By embracing the rhythms and movements based on the natural function of the body and ancient wisdom, we can tap into a deeper sense of harmony and balance, and discover a new way of living that is both joyful and fulfilling. So go ahead and take that first step into the dance studio that is your sitting room, bedroom, kitchen or garden – your body and soul will thank you for it.

"Movement heals the mind, the body and soul. Transforms, and renews you from the inside out. So dance your emotions and channel happy thoughts. Because your brain needs oxygen, fuel and activation. And your state of mind feeds your brain" - Grace E

Grace Ekall

Website: www.habitsthathealstudio.com

Instagram: @habitsthatheal

Podcast: https://5steps3rhythmspodcast.buzzsprout.com s

YouTube: @habitsthatheal2550

Facebook: https://www.facebook.com/HTHMindsetBodyFood

FREE Facebook Group: https://www.facebook.com/groups/habitsthatheal

LinkedIn: https://www.linkedin.com/in/grace-ekall-a929bb15/

Printed in Great Britain
by Amazon

33647832R00044